The Egyptian Collar Mystery

By Mike Dion

Illustrated by Sally Schaedler

Celebration Press
Pearson Learning Group

Contents

Chapter 1

A Building of Secrets

Tracy Marr leaned against the iron fence that surrounded the old mansion. She hugged a box to her chest.

"Here it is," she said excitedly, "Trueheart Mansion, where the Trueheart Egyptian Collection is! I wish we could just skip the other donations and focus on this one. I can't believe Mrs. Trueheart is giving us a golden collar from ancient Egypt!"

"Isn't it really a necklace?" asked her friend Grace Chandler. "Why do they call it a collar anyway?"

3

"It's because an Egyptian collar didn't just circle the neck," explained Noah, Grace's twin brother. "It also covered the top of a person's robe."

"Whatever you call it, it's the most important donation for tomorrow's auction," said Tracy. "Dad says a piece of jewelry from ancient Egypt will make the auction a success for sure."

Tracy's dad was Sergeant Marr of the city police. He was also one of the organizers of the Library Fund auction. The organizers hoped that the auction would raise enough money to build a new library. Many people had donated items to be auctioned. Tracy, Grace, and Noah were helping to collect some of them.

Grace joined Tracy at the fence. "I heard the Truehearts have a special room in that mansion just for the art they collected from Egypt," she said. "Imagine having your own personal one-room museum!"

"And your own tower," added Tracy, staring at the huge, beautiful mansion with its pointed roofs, turrets, and tower.

"And that lawn must take a week to mow," said Noah. "Let's get going, slowpokes! We've only picked up one item so far—that silver vase. What else are we supposed to get?"

"A painting and a quilt," said Tracy. "After that, we'll meet my dad back here at Trueheart Mansion at 5:30. He's going to take the Egyptian collar right to the police station and lock it up to keep it safe."

Tracy started walking down the sidewalk again toward town. "I'd really like to know why Mrs. Trueheart is giving something so valuable for the auction," she continued. "Wouldn't you think she'd want to keep all the pieces in her Egyptian Collection? She's spent so much time and money getting them and displaying them."

"Maybe she likes being interviewed for the newspaper and TV," said Noah with a shrug.

"Maybe she's just being nice!" said Grace. "After all, a new library would do a whole lot of good for this city."

"Yeah, maybe she wants us to name the new library after her!" suggested Noah.

None of these explanations satisfied Tracy, but she put her questions aside for the moment. Their next stop, Archer Reed's painting studio, was downtown on Spring Street, but she wasn't sure just where.

"Help me look for the Reed Gallery sign!" Tracy said as they reached Spring Street. She wove quickly through the sidewalk traffic, trying to read every store sign at once.

"Wait a minute," called Grace. "Look at the bracelet in this shop window!"

"It looks more like an armband to me," said Noah.

"Let me see!" said Tracy.

She peered into the shop window. The thick gold bracelet did look like an ancient Egyptian armband. Some of the other jewelry looked Egyptian, too. One ring was carved with a scarab design. Scarabs, or beetles, were common in ancient Egypt, and jewelry was often crafted in that shape. Just then an elegant hand reached into the window. On it were three amazing rings. The hand placed a hand-lettered *Closed* sign against the back of the display.

"Look at those rings!" breathed Grace.

Tracy was more interested in the woman who belonged to the hand. She darted to the shop door to get a better look, but a man's back blocked her view.

"Tomorrow's the day," she heard him say to the woman inside the shop. "If all goes well tonight, we'll live happily ever after!"

Happily ever after! What was going to happen tonight? He must be speaking to the woman with the rings. Tracy got up on her tiptoes, but she still couldn't see inside. Then Noah tugged on her arm.

"Let's get going!" he prodded. "I see the Reed Gallery sign on the next block!"

The gallery! Tracy's mind returned to the Library Fund auction. The sooner they collected the painting, the sooner they could get the quilt. Then they could go back to the Trueheart Mansion for a real treasure from ancient Egypt!

Noah pointed to the Reed Gallery sign one block down that hung over the sidewalk.

"Archer Reed's studio is over his gallery," said Tracy. "It's on the top floor. That's where we're supposed to pick up the painting he's donating."

Tracy, Grace, and Noah stopped at a door to the side of the gallery. Tracy opened it and discovered a steep staircase. She bolted quickly up the stairs. Grace soon caught up with her, but Noah passed them both on the first landing. Then it became a race. The heavy vase Tracy carried slowed her down, and Grace moved ahead. Their footsteps raised a thunderous clatter in the stairwell.

"Tracy!" Grace called from above.

Tracy looked up. Grace and Noah waited impatiently on the top floor, motioning her to hurry.

"It's about time!" said Grace when Tracy reached the landing, breathing heavily.

Tracy set the vase box down and then drew back as an angry voice rose inside the studio.

"I promised and I deliver what I promise!" roared the voice. "I said I'll get it for you!"

"Sounds like somebody's got trouble," said Noah in a low voice.

Grace nodded and Tracy approached the door, hoping to overhear more. She tripped over the vase box, knocking it against the wall with a bang. Instantly the studio door flew open. A short man in paint-stained clothing stared angrily at them. His scowling face was framed by close-cropped, graying hair.

"Yes?" he demanded.

Tracy gathered her courage. "Mr. Reed?" she asked brightly. "I'm Tracy Marr. We're here to collect the painting you were kind enough to donate to the Library Fund auction."

"Ah!" The man's face changed instantly from angry to cordial. "Yes, yes, come in, come in! You're just in time. I have to be somewhere else in 20 minutes."

Tracy eagerly stepped inside. She'd never been inside a painter's studio before. A huge window in the slanted ceiling let in a dazzle of light. Her eyes were drawn to two unfinished paintings. One was a portrait, and the other, a dancer warming up.

"Wow, fantastic!" breathed Grace. She moved closer to the painting of the dancer.

"You like my work?" asked the painter. "I like to paint people. People are what make the world lively and sparkling! My skill turns even difficult people into beautiful paintings!"

"Imagine what he could do with you, Tracy," teased Noah.

Tracy ignored him. She'd noticed that the telephone was still off the hook. Would the artist continue his strange conversation while they were there? Instead, Archer Reed reached for a flat package leaning against his drawing table.

"I'm donating a splendid painting to the auction," he declared. "A masterpiece—passengers at the train station. Can I trust you to care for it properly?"

He handed the painting, wrapped in plain brown paper, to Noah carefully.

"I'll guard it with my life," said Noah solemnly.

Tracy could tell he was holding back a laugh.

"Good, good, now get going," said Archer Reed. "I'm rushed and busy, busy, busy!"

He glared in Grace's direction. Grace was so fascinated with the painting of the dancer that Tracy had to tap her shoulder to get her attention.

The three filed past Reed as he picked up the telephone and shooed them out. They were barely in the hall when he slammed the door behind them.

"Whew!" said Tracy. "I feel like he just lifted me up and blew me out the door! He's just like a human hurricane!"

"He's a bag of wind, all right," agreed Noah.

"I wish I could see the painting in that package," said Grace longingly. "If it's anything like his unfinished dancer, I know it's beautiful."

"Didn't you hear the man?" asked Noah in mock surprise. "His painting is splendid, a masterpiece!"

Tracy giggled. She bent to pick up the boxed vase again, listening to the sound of Archer Reed's voice as he resumed his phone conversation. It sounded like an argument to her.

"I tell you, I'll be there tonight!" the painter shouted. "I'll get it tonight if I have to steal it!"

Chapter 2

Trueheart Mansion

"What is he talking about stealing?" whispered Tracy in frustration. She leaned toward the door.

Grace shook her head gravely.

"It's none of our business, Miss Snoop," Noah scolded. "Our business is to get to that quilt shop. Remember the quilt donation?"

He plunged down the stairs. Grace took off rapidly after him.

"But what will he get tonight?" wailed Tracy as she barreled after them. "I really want to know!"

"A pizza!" called Noah.

"A fever!" laughed Grace.

"A headache!" shouted Noah.

"A good night's sleep!" shrieked Grace, doubling over with laughter.

"Be serious!" protested Tracy. She couldn't stand it when the twins got silly. "Archer Reed actually suggested stealing something!"

"Oh, how do you know he wasn't just blowing hot air?" scoffed Noah. "I'll bet that the only thing that man takes seriously is himself!"

"Well," said Tracy, unconvinced.

"Forget it, Tracy!" coaxed Grace. "We've got something more exciting than Mr. Archer Reed on our schedule for today!"

"Yeah, keep your eyes on the prize, Tracy," said Noah. "We'll get the quilt first. Then we'll get to see the Trueheart Mansion and an Egyptian treasure!"

"All right, all right," said Tracy with a sigh. "I give up. Unless we hear about some fantastic robbery," she added.

"The great pizza robbery," said Noah.

"The great headache robbery!" shrieked Grace. "That's what he'll get tonight, a headache!"

"If he spends any time with you, he probably will," muttered Tracy.

They found the quilt shop and picked up the donation of a handmade quilt. Then they returned to the Trueheart Mansion, grumbling about the bulky packages they had to carry. However, they forgot their complaints as they passed through the tall iron gates to the elegant mansion.

"My dad says this place used to be on the edge of town a hundred years ago," said Tracy. "Now it looks caged in."

"A hundred years ago the Trueheart family was traveling back and forth to Egypt by steamship," said Noah.

"And finding and buying treasures like the collar they're donating to us," added Grace.

A brisk wind scattered fallen leaves as the three started up the wide driveway. Tracy shivered from the cold wind and from excitement. Was it possible they'd have a chance to view the contents of the famous Egyptian Room?

"I've passed this place a thousand times," Tracy said, "but I never thought I'd ever get to see the inside! I know we're here to get the Library Fund auction's most valuable donation, but I feel like we're stepping back into another time!"

The wind blew harder as they climbed the mansion's steps, and Noah had to struggle to support the painting.

"I'm getting cold!" complained Grace.

Swirling leaves hit Tracy's legs as she reached for the doorknocker. "Look," she exclaimed, "it's a mummy!"

The brass figure of a mummy hung on the door, a knocker ring suspended from its hands. Tracy lifted the heavy ring and let it fall once. Its loud warning echoed, announcing their arrival.

"It's loud enough to wake the dead," Noah teased.

Did the Trueheart collection include any mummies? Tracy shivered again as the door opened.

Chapter 3

Presentation of the Golden Collar

A young woman stood by the open door and eyed them expectantly. Tracy heard Grace's murmured appreciation of the necklace that circled the woman's throat.

"Are you the children from the library auction?" the woman asked.

"Yes," said Tracy. "I'm Sergeant Marr's daughter Tracy, and these are my friends Grace and Noah Chandler."

"I am Prudence Trueheart," said the young woman. Please come inside. My aunt has been waiting for you."

17

The woman stepped back and motioned for the three to follow her inside. Something sparkled on her fingers, and Grace nudged Tracy's shoulder.

"Did you recognize those rings?" Grace whispered.

Tracy hadn't noticed the rings. The minute she stepped into the grand entrance hall, she began looking around for Egyptian statues.

It was as cold inside Trueheart Mansion as it was outside, and darker, too. No sunlight shone into the mansion's entrance hall. The wind had blown a few leaves inside the open door.

"You may leave your packages here," said Prudence.

The three set the packaged vase, painting, and quilt down on a large carved bench. They all kept their jackets on. Tracy and Grace gawked at the stained glass window over the landing at the top of the double staircase. Even Noah gave a low whistle. The whole place looked like a museum!

"Come into the drawing room," said Prudence. "My aunt will speak to you there."

When she turned left into a large room, Tracy was right on her heels. Maybe it was warmer in the drawing room!

It did seem warmer. The late afternoon October sun sent golden light through the long windows. Tracy noticed a silver tea service and platter of sandwiches on a small table. So tea parties didn't happen just in books!

"Look who's come to tea," whispered Noah.

"Who?" asked Grace.

Tracy turned toward the fireplace, where welcome flames danced. Three people clustered around it for warmth. One of them was Archer Reed!

"Here are the children from the Library Fund auction, Aunt Edith," announced Prudence.

"At last," said a commanding voice.

Prudence recited their names while Tracy studied the woman who approached. So this was Mrs. Trueheart, the woman who had decided to part with a valuable piece of art from her private collection! She was tall and proud looking. Silver hair did not soften her stern face.

"Thank you so much for donating an Egyptian piece to the Library Fund auction!" said Tracy. "It will certainly raise a great deal of money for our new library building!"

"It should," said Mrs. Trueheart, smiling slightly. "It's priceless to me, as it's been in my family for more than a century. Let me introduce my guests, also auction donors—the painter, Archer Reed—"

"We've met," said the painter. "Is my painting safe, young man?" he asked, addressing Noah.

"Safe and sound in the hall," replied Noah gravely.

"Excellent, excellent," said Reed.

"And this is my niece's friend Ken Jury, otherwise known as Jury the Clown," said Mrs. Trueheart, in a tone of voice that sounded as though she'd meant to say "Jury, the Slimy Toad."

Tracy smiled at Jury the Clown, who looked like a friendly teacher.

"Hi, kids," he said. "Call me Jury. I'm my own donation. The highest bidder will have Jury the Clown as entertainment at his or her next party."

Where had Tracy heard that voice before?

"My niece Prudence lives here in the mansion," continued Mrs. Trueheart. "She claims to believe I need looking after." She cast an offended smile in poor Prudence's direction.

"Whew," breathed Noah, close to Tracy's ear. "Prudence deserves a medal for bravery!"

"There's another guest to greet," said Jury, "the dancing half of my act. Docket, say hello!"

A little dog rose up on its hind legs. It danced and yipped "hello."

"That's enough foolishness," said Mrs. Trueheart. "Let's get to the purpose of this celebration."

Mrs. Trueheart smiled stiffly at Tracy, Grace, and Noah. "Well," thought Tracy, "I'd be less than completely happy, too, giving away such a valuable piece of art."

"Bring me the box, Prudence!" commanded Mrs. Trueheart.

"Don't you have it with you, Aunt Edith?" Prudence asked anxiously. "You were carrying it when we returned here from the Egyptian Room."

Tracy looked from one Trueheart to the other. How could they lose track of a box containing an ancient Egyptian collar?

"It's on the tea table, Edith," said Archer Reed.

"Oh, of course," said Mrs. Trueheart.

She stalked to the table to get the wooden box. Docket stood on his hind legs again and yipped twice.

"He's begging," said Mrs. Trueheart with disapproval.

"No, he sees the box," explained Jury. "He likes to open things with his nose. He opens boxes as part of our act."

Mrs. Trueheart snorted with displeasure. Docket walked toward her on his hind legs, begging for the box, but Mrs. Trueheart turned to Tracy.

"How will you ensure the collar's safety?" she demanded.

"You needn't worry," Tracy assured her. "My dad's a sergeant on the police force. After he meets us here, we'll go straight to the police station and lock the collar up. It will be kept under constant guard."

A strange expression crossed Mrs. Trueheart's face. Little Docket yipped again. "Take that dog away!" she snapped.

Grace picked up Docket, and Tracy edged closer to the box. Another minute and she'd be able to see and touch a piece of jewelry that someone had worn in ancient Egypt— maybe someone in the Pharaoh's palace! She held her breath in anticipation, but Mrs. Trueheart didn't move. The woman stood like a statue, gripping the box and clenching her teeth nervously.

"What are you waiting for, Edith?" asked Archer Reed impatiently. "Didn't you ask Jury and me here precisely to make a ceremony of this occasion?"

"Yes, indeed I did." Mrs. Trueheart lifted her chin. "It's just that—"

"It's just that she doesn't want to give away something so precious," Noah whispered.

"Is there a problem, Aunt Edith?" asked Prudence nervously.

Mrs. Trueheart shook her head. "No," she said in a firm voice, "it's nothing." She gestured to Tracy with a queenly air. "Young lady, I am proud to donate this marvelous piece of art to a worthy cause. I present you with a golden collar from the Valley of the Pharaohs."

Chapter 4

Missing!

Tracy imagined she heard trumpets and felt the heat of a desert sun as she accepted the box from Mrs. Trueheart. Grace and Noah crowded around her, as did Prudence, Jury, and Archer Reed. Docket stretched out from Grace's arms, and with a quick nudge he pushed the lid open with his foxy nose. Tracy held her breath.

The box was empty!

"Nothing's in there!" exclaimed Grace.

She startled Docket, who wriggled from her grasp.

"What?" cried Prudence sharply, grabbing the box. "Aunt Edith, the collar is missing!"

Mrs. Trueheart jerked a hand over her heart and collapsed onto a chair. Prudence passed the box back to Tracy and rushed to her aunt's side.

"Has she fainted?" asked Jury. "I'll get some water."

He headed for the pitcher of water on the tea table. Grace adjusted a pillow under Mrs. Trueheart's head while Noah fanned her face with a magazine. Archer Reed folded his arms and watched everyone else attend their stricken hostess.

Tracy examined the empty box. It had no hidden trick drawers, no lock. Could Mrs. Trueheart have somehow forgotten to place the collar inside?

Mrs. Trueheart stirred, her eyelids fluttering.

"My collar!" she moaned.

"We'll find it, Aunt Edith!" said Prudence, but her voice trembled. "We have to," she added in a whisper.

"We have to," Tracy echoed as Grace and Noah examined the empty box.

She felt sick at the thought of tomorrow's auction. If the Egyptian collar were lost, the auction might be a complete failure! Docket seemed to sense everybody's distress. He yipped, and Jury cradled him, crooning.

Archer Reed ended his own dramatic silence.

"Which Egyptian collar is missing?" he inquired. "Was it the one you wore for the portrait I painted?"

Mrs. Trueheart lifted her hand to her forehead. "No," she answered faintly, closing her eyes.

"Then it was the collar you wore to the opening performance at the City Opera House," said Reed.

"It was neither!" Mrs. Trueheart snapped.

"I don't remember seeing more than two collars in your Egyptian Room," said Jury, as if he were thinking aloud.

"That's because I put the donated collar into the box!" barked Mrs. Trueheart. She sat up and turned to her niece. "Prudence, stop fussing about me. It was just the shock."

Tracy ventured a question. "When did you put the collar in the box, Mrs. Trueheart?" she asked.

"Yesterday," said Mrs. Trueheart. "I left the box locked in the Egyptian Room until today—until just before I invited my guests upstairs to view the collection."

"Did you check inside the box?" asked Tracy.

Mrs. Trueheart's face turned red. "I looked at the collar about three o'clock when I unlocked the room," she declared frostily, glaring at Prudence, Jury, and Archer Reed. Her accusation was clear.

Tracy considered the situation. Supposedly the theft had occurred within about the last hour and a half. If Mrs. Trueheart was correct, one of the other three adults was the culprit, or guilty party, so the collar could still be somewhere in the mansion.

"We should begin a search for the collar," Tracy said earnestly. "If we don't find it, you can report it missing to my dad. He should be here in half an hour."

"That doesn't give us a lot of time to find the missing collar, does it?" murmured Archer Reed.

Tracy wondered why Mrs. Trueheart looked so horrified. Even if she believed one of her guests had stolen the collar, maybe she didn't want to file an official police report.

Tracy looked quickly over the other adult faces. Was one of them a thief? Would Mrs. Trueheart's own niece steal from her, and if so, why? Jury the Clown was so friendly that Tracy didn't want him to be the culprit. Archer Reed seemed arrogant, but he was a wonderful painter. How could he stoop so low as to steal something!

Tracy felt almost as horrified as Mrs. Trueheart looked. She hoped the mention of her police-sergeant father would cause the thief to think twice and "find" the collar. They really had to find the collar. The success of the auction depended upon it!

Archer Reed wore a faint scowl. "You have an important collection, Edith," he stated. "There has been a great deal of publicity about it lately, especially since word got out about your donation to the auction. Perhaps we should make certain nothing else is missing."

"That isn't necessary—" began Mrs. Trueheart.

"Yes, it is," interrupted Prudence firmly. "We should make certain and right now, Aunt Edith."

Mrs. Trueheart struggled to her feet.

"You're right, of course," she said. "Come with me, all of you."

"The Egyptian Collection!" whispered Tracy, clutching Grace's arm. "We're going to get to see it after all!"

Exchanging thrilled glances, the three trooped silently with the others through the cold entrance hall and up to the second floor. They passed without speaking beneath the jewel-toned window with its stained-glass flowers.

"The tower room!" exclaimed Grace.

Tracy held her breath as Mrs. Trueheart unlocked the tower-room door with a key hanging from a chain around her neck. Was that the only key to the Egyptian Collection?

"Go inside," Mrs. Trueheart commanded. "I will follow you."

They all filed inside. Tracy forgot the missing collar as the room's mysterious silence surrounded her. Did that silence follow the ancient treasures in the room all the way from Egypt?

She heard Grace sigh with pleasure and Noah whisper, "Wow," but Tracy couldn't speak. She turned slowly to take it all in—the glass display cases that guarded the small treasures, statues carved for Pharaohs, the mummy case that once held the body of a person who had lived so long ago.

"Fascinating, isn't it?" said Archer Reed.

Tracy heard the edge in his voice and wondered if he was fascinated enough with the treasures to steal the collar.

Tracy turned her attention back to the reason they were there. Suddenly Mrs. Trueheart marched to the center of the room and glared at each of them in turn.

"You are all locked in," she announced. "Nothing else will leave this room."

"Locked in with a clown dog," whispered Noah.

Grace stifled a nervous giggle, but Tracy was a little scared. Was she scared of the mummy case, or of being locked in with a probable thief? Now that she had seen the Egyptian Room, Tracy doubted the collar could have been mislaid by accident.

Prudence bent over a display case. "Where was the collar, Aunt Edith?" she asked. "I mean, before you decided to donate it?"

"In the case!" snapped Mrs. Trueheart.

Tracy, Grace, and Noah looked in the display case. There were two collars, some rings, hair combs, and even a little pot of ancient makeup. But there were no empty spaces.

Prudence brushed a bit of dust off the case, and Tracy saw the rings on her fingers. Grace was right! Those were the same rings—and the same hand— they'd seen downtown! Prudence was the woman in the jewelry shop!

Now Tracy realized why Jury's voice had sounded familiar. He must be the man who blocked her view of the shop!

"Here's the collar I thought you meant to donate," observed Prudence, "and I don't see any empty spaces."

"I moved things around," said Mrs. Trueheart.

"When exactly did you do that?" asked Jury.

Mrs. Trueheart glared at him. "When I put the collar in the box!" she barked.

Then Tracy remembered the words she'd overheard at the jewelry shop. Were those words a clue to the mystery of the missing collar? She drew Grace and Noah aside.

"Do you remember what we saw at the jewelry shop?" Tracy asked.

"Of course!" whispered Grace. "I told you I recognized those rings! It was Prudence's hand we saw in that shop!"

Tracy agreed, "And I think that was Jury standing in the door saying 'If all goes well tonight, we'll live happily ever after.'"

The three friends exchanged serious looks.

Noah said, "It sounds like Jury was talking about what would happen after stealing the collar!"

"Not Jury, he's honest!" protested Grace. "Look how terrific he is with that dog!"

"He trained that dog to open boxes," Noah reminded her. "Maybe Docket is his accomplice!"

Tracy glanced at Jury. Carrying Docket, he stood beside Prudence as she went over every inch of the second display case. Prudence looked desperate.

"Do you think Prudence and Jury stole the collar?" whispered Tracy. "She looks frightened."

"Maybe she knows Jury stole it," said Noah.

"Or she's afraid he did," said Grace. "Prudence didn't steal anything. She looks as if she's going to cry!"

"That doesn't mean anything," said Noah.

"Hush," said Grace. "You're both so suspicious."

She turned her back on Noah and Tracy. Tracy didn't blame her. She didn't want it to be Prudence either, or Jury. She just wanted to find the collar.

Prudence appealed to the group, "Please help me look for the collar!" she pleaded. "Maybe Aunt Edith accidentally dropped it!"

"Oh sure," muttered Noah. "Drop a heavy piece of ancient Egyptian jewelry without noticing?"

But he helped as everybody except Mrs. Trueheart searched the room.

Tracy circled the tall, slim statue of a cat. "Can you tell us about the missing collar?" she whispered to it.

The statue was so dignified and mysterious that she almost thought it did know the secret. But if it did, it wasn't saying anything.

"This is useless," maintained Archer Reed. "Useless, useless, useless. The collar isn't here."

"How does he know?" whispered Grace to Noah. "Did he take it?"

Tracy felt the tension in the room heighten. She drew closer to Grace and Noah.

36

"Reed must know a lot of art dealers," she speculated to her friends. "Maybe he promised to sell the collar to a crooked dealer. Maybe that's the one he was talking to on the phone. Remember, he said, 'I'll get it tonight!' He said he'd steal something if he had to!"

Grace and Noah raised their eyebrows at the same minute and turned their eyes toward Archer Reed. But Prudence captured Tracy's attention. Prudence's right hand was playing with the necklace she wore, as though it could comfort her. Why did she look so anxious? Was that a look of guilt?

"The collar isn't anywhere in this room!" said Prudence, her voice filled with dread. "Could you have mislaid it downstairs, Aunt Edith? We should search the rest of the house."

"Mislaid my own collar?" repeated Mrs. Trueheart. "No, enough searching! Downstairs with you all! I must call the insurance company, and I want you all where I can see you!"

If looks were fire, they all would have been scorched. Tracy wondered what Mrs. Trueheart would say to Dad when he arrived, and whether he would search the whole house. But mostly she wondered who was hiding the truth!

Chapter 5

Solving the Puzzle

Downstairs again, no one put a log on the dying fire. No one offered food, even though Noah's and Docket's eyes were fixed on the sandwiches.

"I'm cold," complained Grace.

Tracy was, too, even though she and Grace huddled together in one overstuffed chair. Noah perched on its arm. Jury and Prudence sat on a small sofa nearby, with Docket sharing their laps. Mrs. Trueheart hadn't phoned yet. She and Archer Reed were engaged in a fierce but quiet argument across the room.

Tracy looked at the portrait on the wall of a younger Mrs. Trueheart. She wore an Egyptian-style robe and jewelry from the Egyptian Collection—including a collar. Had Archer Reed painted the portrait?

"I should never have agreed to marry you!" Prudence wailed to Jury.

Tracy forgot all about the portrait. She listened eagerly as Prudence continued.

"I should never have planned to move away from the mansion!" She was staring at Reed and her angry aunt. "You don't know Aunt Edith the way I do! She loses her good judgment when she gets upset!" Prudence buried her face in Jury's shoulder.

Noah bent close to the girls. "Maybe those two stole the collar so they could afford to get married and move away," he suggested. "Remember, they said, 'Tomorrow's the day.'"

"No, wait!" said Tracy, as a new explanation popped into her head. "Maybe what I overheard wasn't about stealing the collar!" She raised her voice. "When do you two plan to get married?" she asked Prudence and Jury.

"We were going to elope tomorrow," said Jury. "My law practice is really picking up, and so is Prudence's business. We decided that now is a good time to get married."

"Law practice!" said Noah.

"Business?" said Tracy.

"I thought you were a clown!" protested Grace.

"I am—on weekends," said Jury with a grin.

"Weekday lawyer, weekend clown," he went on. "I like clowning, and it was a way to make a little money during law school. Now I have a successful law practice, and Prudence sells the jewelry she makes in a little shop downtown. She's getting quite a reputation! I won't be surprised if one day she becomes a famous jewelry designer!"

"You make the jewelry you sell?" exclaimed Grace. "You made those rings, and the bracelet in the window? They're awesome!"

"Thank you," said Prudence unhappily.

"We're sitting pretty," said Jury, casting an affectionate glance at Prudence's sorrowful face.

"There goes their motive for stealing," Tracy murmured to Grace and Noah. "That is, if they're telling the truth."

"That leaves Archer Reed," said Grace.

From across the room Reed's voice rose steadily, "Just return it, Edith! It's my very best work and I have a buyer for it! Must I get the law involved?"

"Don't threaten me, Archer!" spat Mrs. Trueheart. "I gave you your start! You painted that portrait before anyone knew who you were!"

"I never gave it to you!" retorted Reed. "That painting was a commission, but you never paid me!"

Prudence jumped up, upsetting Docket. "Stop it! Aunt Edith is upset enough!" she cried. "Discuss your painting later!"

"We'll discuss it now," said Reed. "Maybe I'll tell that policeman when he materializes."

"Maybe you took the collar, Archer!" accused Prudence. "Return it, and she'll return your painting!"

Docket went over to Mrs. Trueheart. "Get that horrible dog away!" she said. "He took the collar! He opened the box and took it away!"

"Oh, yeah?" said Jury, leaping to his feet. "And took it where exactly?"

As the four adults continued to argue, Tracy clapped her hands to her head. "Reed, Reed," she muttered. "He was going to get something tonight. Was it the collar? Or the painting?"

"He said he'd get it even if he had to steal it," said Grace. "He must have been talking about the collar! After all, it's the collar that's missing!"

"But what about that painting?" argued Noah. "It sounds as if she stole it from him!"

"Something weird is going on," Tracy said. "Why would Mrs. Trueheart put the collar in an unlocked box? And why would she leave it lying around until we got here, especially if she thought Docket might take it?"

The sound of the heavy brass knocker halted both the argument and the speculation.

"Dad!" said Tracy.

She ran to the front door and opened it. "You'd better come in," she said. "We have a problem here."

"Not the Egyptian collar?" asked Dad. When Tracy nodded, he added, "I knew it was too good to be true. Brrr, it's cold in this hall!"

"Why was Mrs. Trueheart's house so cold?" Tracy asked herself. Then she wondered if Mrs. Trueheart could afford to heat it! Maybe she didn't have any money but wouldn't admit it.

42

Maybe she was too proud to sell her mansion, or part of her famous Egyptian collection! But then why donate a collar to the auction?

The adults looked at Tracy's dad warily as he entered the drawing room.

"This is my father, Sergeant Marr," said Tracy. "Dad, this is Mrs. Trueheart. The collar she was going to donate is missing."

"That's serious," said Dad. "Do you want to report the loss officially, Mrs. Trueheart?"

Mrs. Trueheart's face went gray. She opened her mouth and closed it again. Suddenly Tracy remembered something Mrs. Trueheart had said, and it all came together. She knew the answer to the mystery of the missing collar!

43

"You never meant to donate the collar, did you, Mrs. Trueheart?" she asked quietly. "You were going to say it was stolen and collect money from your insurance company."

Mrs. Trueheart gasped. Prudence put an arm around her.

"Tracy, insurance fraud is a serious crime," warned Dad. "You can't accuse someone lightly."

"I'm afraid your daughter might be right," said Prudence unhappily. "We were just upstairs searching in the Egyptian Room. I know the pieces there almost as well as Aunt Edith does, and there is nothing missing. Nothing has been stolen—or donated. Isn't that right, Aunt Edith?" she asked. "Please tell the truth."

Mrs. Trueheart hung her head like an ashamed child. "I didn't want to do it," she said. "But I didn't want to sell the family collection or the Trueheart house. I've lived here all my life. Every year expenses go up. I didn't know what to do. I don't have the money to pay all the bills."

"That's why it's so cold in here!" exclaimed Grace.

Mrs. Trueheart nodded and burst into tears. Prudence pulled her closer.

"You were planning to file a false claim of theft, Ma'am," said Sergeant Marr. "That's a crime—the same as stealing."

"But she didn't actually do it!" protested Prudence.

"She would have let one of us be taken for a thief!" said Archer Reed. "She'd sacrifice our reputations—no, steal them—so she could collect insurance money! And what about my painting?"

Prudence looked desperately at Jury. He straightened, and his relaxed expression disappeared. Now he was all lawyer.

"I'd like to consult with my client, please," he said. He took Mrs. Trueheart's arm and led her and Prudence toward the back of the room.

"I guess you were right, Tracy," said Dad. "But it's a good thing Mrs. Trueheart's lawyer is present."

"How did you figure it out, Tracy?" asked Grace.

"First," said Tracy, "it's cold in here! Next, Mrs. Trueheart has the only key to the Egyptian Room and wears it on a chain around her neck. How could anybody else get into that room? Then Prudence said the collar her aunt was going to donate was still in the Egyptian Collection.

"After that Archer Reed accused Mrs. Trueheart of keeping one of his paintings, and I began to think she couldn't be trusted.

"Then I remembered that she didn't want us to keep on searching for the collar—but she did want to call her insurance company!"

Prudence, Jury, and Mrs. Trueheart returned.

"Sergeant," said Jury, "Mrs. Trueheart will return to Archer Reed the portrait she says he gave her."

"She never paid me for it," growled Reed. "That's a museum quality portrait, and I have a buyer for it!"

Jury held up his hand. "No more talk, Archer," he said. "You can take it tonight." He turned to Sergeant Marr. "Mrs. Trueheart will donate an Egyptian collar to the Library Fund auction, as promised."

"All right!" exclaimed Noah.

He and Grace exchanged a smile, and Tracy let out a deep breath. She'd been afraid the auction would have to go on without the donation, in spite of the failure of Mrs. Trueheart's scheme.

"Mrs. Trueheart will also seek a buyer for part of the Egyptian Collection so she can pay her bills," continued Jury. "And after Prudence and I marry, we'll live here at Trueheart Mansion with her. Perhaps together we three can keep the Trueheart home intact."

"Poor Docket," murmured Noah in a low voice.

"You're a lucky woman, Mrs. Trueheart," said Sergeant Marr. "I hope you deserve these good people."

Mrs. Trueheart looked ashamed. "I'll try to," she said in a low voice. "I'm ashamed at what I was thinking. I apologize to you all."

Prudence took her aunt's hand. "Give me the key to the Egyptian Room, Aunt Edith," she said gently. "It's time to donate a collar to the auction."

Slowly Mrs. Trueheart removed the chain with its key from around her neck. Her lip quivered as she handed it to Prudence, who smiled for the first time that day.

"I'll be just a minute," she promised.

No one spoke until Prudence returned, carrying a five-strand collar of gold beads from her aunt's collection. The collar gleamed as Prudence handed it to her aunt. Mrs. Trueheart placed the collar gently into Tracy's open palms.

"It's beautiful!" breathed Grace.

"Fit for a Pharaoh," declared Noah.

Tracy thought the collar was beautiful, but it wasn't Mrs. Trueheart's real treasure. That was her family—Prudence, Jury, and Docket, the ones who loved her.